Helena Haraštová & Pavla Hanáčková & Michaela Bergmannová

How Kids Celebrate Holidays Around the World

ALBATROS

THANKSGIVING
32

HANUKKAH
34

HALLOWEEN
30

DAY OF
THE DEAD
28

CARNIVAL
8

INTI RAYMI
20

N

W   E

S

EASTER
14

GIRLS' DAY
10

PURIM
12

EID AL-ADHA
24

DIWALI
26

VESAK
18

TIMKAT
6

KUMBH
MELA
16

EID AL-FITR
22

Why do we have holidays?

Every society commemorates events that have deep meaning for its people. This is done regularly, usually at the same time each year. We call such commemorations holidays. Some are connected with nature, others with religion. At holiday time, people practice various customs and rituals, some of which have existed for hundreds of years!

Let's celebrate the holidays!

Happy Halloween!

Happy Diwali!

Look at that skeleton!

What do people celebrate?

There are many reasons to hold a celebration. Some holidays honor a historical event or mark an important point in the development of a religion. The Jewish holiday Hanukkah, for instance, celebrates the victory of the Jews over their enemies in the second century BCE. The Hindu holiday Vesak commemorates three events in the life of the Buddha. At Easter, Christians all over the world commemorate the Resurrection of Jesus Christ. Some holidays are connected with nature—the Peruvian holiday Inti Raymi, for instance, is associated with the winter solstice, when people celebrate the end of the period of short days and long nights. Although holidays are celebrated in all kinds of ways, there are a few things they all have in common, notably time spent with loved ones, lots of fun, and respect for tradition.

How old are holidays?

Holidays have existed since time immemorial. Many festivities are so old that we have no written record of their precise origins. Long ago, holidays were mostly associated with the seasons (like the coming of spring), agriculture (like the harvest), religion (like the birth of an important saint), or important events in the lives of our ancestors. Certain holiday rituals and customs have changed over time. Some, however, have been passed all the way down to today's generations. Perhaps you practice them yourself.

Happy Inti Raymi!

It's Girl's Day!

This is a menorah!

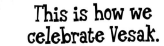

This is how we celebrate Vesak.

Celebrations Around the world

Some holidays, particularly religious ones, are celebrated in similar ways all over the world. But others are miles apart in terms of how they are celebrated, even though they mark practically the same thing. It all depends on how the given event is viewed in a particular country. Take All Souls Day, when many Europeans solemnly remember their dead. In Mexico, they take a different attitude to life and death. Their day of remembrance is a joyous event that is lively and colorful. And in that spirit, let's take a trip and learn how children mark holidays around the world!

Dilla celebrates TIMKAT

MELKAM TIMKAT! MY NAME'S **DILLA** AND I LIVE IN ETHIOPIA. IT'S JANUARY, AND PEOPLE ALL OVER THE COUNTRY ARE CELEBRATING TIMKAT, WHEN WE COMMEMORATE JESUS'S BAPTISM IN THE RIVER JORDAN. WE ETHIOPIANS WERE AMONG THE FIRST NATIONS TO ADOPT CHRISTIANITY.

9 Crosses

Ethiopia is a country with a very old church of its own. We still observe many interesting religious traditions that occur nowhere else in the world. We also have our own cross.

1 Coffee

Ethiopia is one of the places from which coffee originates, and it's still very popular here. It is drunk in small, colorful cups.

2 Tabots

During Timkat, I like to take part in the ceremonial procession, which is led by a priest with a tabot on his head. A tabot is a chest that symbolizes the Ark of the Covenant. We hold our priest in high esteem, which is why he walks on carpet and a deacon holds a parasol over him.

THIS IS
DILLA

3 Waterside celebration

The procession ends at a nearby lake, where the faithful pray and affirm their baptism. The night before, families have picnics on the shore, lit by oil lamps. This is the part of Timkat that I like best.

8 Musicians

Everyone who is able takes part in the procession, as it's an unforgettable occasion! Pilgrims are accompanied by musicians playing African drums, bells, and pipes, making the procession even merrier.

7 Unforgettable experiences

Celebrating this festival is a really unique experience. No wonder people from all over the world come to Ethiopia and enjoy watching the ceremonial procession!

6 Festive meals

During the Timkat holiday our family always comes together for a celebratory meal. This includes *wat*—a traditional Ethiopian stew, which we eat with injera bread.

colorful parasols

Ethiopian coffee

priest with a tabot

5 The Archangel Michael

The third and greatest day of the celebrations is dedicated to the Archangel Michael, Ethiopia's favorite saint.

4 Traditional clothing

Timkat is very important to us, so we wear special clothing during this festival. Traditional all-white dresses prevail, sometimes embroidered with ornaments or decorated with a colorful sash. Women drape their heads or shoulders in a white scarf.

Miguel celebrates CARNIVAL

OLÁ! I'M **MIGUEL** AND I LIVE IN BRAZIL. MY CITY, RIO DE JANEIRO, IS FAMOUS FOR ITS MAGNIFICENT CARNIVAL, WHICH IS HELD ON ASH WEDNESDAY EVERY YEAR. DO YOU KNOW WHAT I ENJOY ABOUT IT MOST? THE UNIQUE MIX OF PEOPLE, COLORS, SOUNDS, CHRISTIAN AND NATIVE AMERICAN SYMBOLS, AND EUPHORIA WHEREVER YOU TURN!

9 The word *carnival*

The word *carnival* is of Latin origin: *carn* means 'meat,' *levare* means 'put away.' So at this time we fast and do not eat meat. The fast begins on Ash Wednesday, the very day that Carnival celebrations start.

1 Costumes

It's impossible to imagine Carnival without its huge variety of masks and costumes! There are many special outfits and makeup in all colors. Some costumes are made of feathers, while others are inspired by indigenous Brazilian patterns.

beautiful costumes

2 Street bands

Carnival keeps the ears of spectators very busy, as well as their eyes. Numerous bands play in the streets, mostly on brass instruments.

3 Carnival queen and King Momo

The Carnival festivities begin with the arrival of King Momo and his queen. On the first day of Carnival, the mayor symbolically hands the key to the city over to the well-built actor playing King Momo.

8

8 Competition

Carnival includes a competition for children's dance groups, too. I'd like to take part in it next year, so I'd better start practicing.

7 Beach parties

In the evening, after Carnival, we go to the city beach, where we continue to talk and dance, meet our friends, and feast our eyes on the fantastic firework display.

6 The samba

In Rio's Carnival parade, it's traditional to dance the samba, a Latin American dance filled with sun, optimism, and *joie de vivre*.

samba dancers

5 Samba schools

People dance samba in the streets of Rio all year-round, but when the Carnival parade is in progress, different samba schools compete against one another. Pupils have a chance to show what they have learned in front of thousands of spectators. And it's not just professionals and celebrities who take part—poor people do, too.

THIS IS
MIGUEL

4 Allegorical cars

See that beautifully decorated car? It's the highlight of the parade. Of ingenious design, it is powered either manually or by an engine. In many cases, costumed dancers stand on top, showing off their moves.

Saki celebrates GIRLS' DAY

KONNICHIWA! I'M **SAKI**, AND I'D LIKE TO WELCOME YOU TO JAPAN. IT'S MARCH 3RD, WHEN WE CELEBRATE DOLL'S DAY, OTHERWISE KNOWN AS GIRLS' DAY. ON THIS DAY, FAMILIES PRAY FOR OUR LITTLE GIRLS' GOOD HEALTH AND HAPPINESS, AND BOYS DON'T MISS OUT—THEY HAVE THEIR OWN DAY IN MAY.

9 Rice cakes

As part of the Girls' Day celebrations we eat sweet biscuits and cakes made from rice.

1 Little girls

In the past, many Japanese died of disease at a very young age. This explains the tradition of relatives encouraging their children (girls and boys) to remain healthy. Today we simply celebrate being together with our loved ones.

2 Dolls on a red carpet

In mid-February we display in our homes—on a tiered platform covered with red carpet—dolls representing the emperor, the empress, samurais, servants, ladies of the court, and musicians. These are placed on five to seven different levels, and there are strict rules as to where each doll belongs and what it is complemented with.

sakura

THIS IS
SAKI

3 A lovely day spent with parents

During the holiday, we visit a shrine with our parents. Then our parents wish us a happy life and give us a present.

8 Saké

It is traditional for adults to drink saké, made from fermented rice.

7 Golden screen

Behind the emperor and empress, who are on the top level, a golden screen is a must, as it symbolizes the throne. The emperor holds a baton, the empress a fan. To each side of the imperial couple is a lamp, and there are two vases between them.

6 Clam soup

A salty soup containing clams is another traditional Girls' Day dish. Shells that fit together perfectly symbolize a happy couple.

clam soup

Japanese delicacies

5 Paper dolls

In certain parts of the country we still observe the ritual of releasing paper dolls into the water. In the past, people believed that evil spirits, disease, and ill fortune would float away with them.

4 Kimono

The kimono is a traditional Japanese garment worn mostly by women, but also sometimes by men. Not only do we dress our dolls in kimonos, but we often wear them ourselves. They are made in countless variations so that every woman and girl can choose one she likes.

Aaron celebrates PURIM

PURIM SAMEACH! WELCOME TO ISRAEL. MY NAME'S **AARON**, AND I'M DRESSED AS MORDECHAI, A BRAVE JEW WHO LIVED LONG AGO. WE COMMEMORATE HIS HEROISM TOGETHER WITH THAT OF HIS NIECE ESTHER DURING PURIM, THE FUNNEST HOLIDAY I KNOW!

10 Synagogue

Jews regularly gather at the synagogue to pray. At Purim, the Book of Esther is read aloud; Jews must listen to it twice.

1 Haman's ears

Another reference to Haman is made with Haman's ears. They're not real ears, of course—they're triangular pastries with a sweet filling.

2 Sweets as gifts

We children like to take baskets filled with food, drink, and sweets to our friends. But we must remember that women give presents to women, and men to men.

3 Purim

Using the Purim ratchet is the most fun of all! When the story of Esther is read aloud, its unpleasant sound rings out every time we hear the name of the hated Haman.

Moneybox

4 Gifts for the poor

During Purim it is our duty to give our help to anyone who asks for it, without questioning whether they are truly suffering as they claim. Everyone should give to at least two people in need.

9 Coins

Long ago, when the Temple in Jerusalem was still standing, the faithful would put a half-shekel in its money box. We still put small coins in a synagogue's money box today, either when the Book of Esther is being read or a day earlier.

8 Vegetarian food

As Esther didn't eat any meat at the royal palace, so as not to reveal her Jewish origins, in her honor some people eat no meat during today's feast. The only flesh you find on their plate is fish.

7 The Book of Esther

Today we celebrate the deliverance of Jews, whose lives were once in great danger in Persia. Haman, a wicked leader, intended to have the Jews killed, but the wise, kindly queen Esther, herself a Jew, talked him out of this, with Mordechai's help. We can read this story in the Book of Esther, a part of our holy Torah.

The Book of Esther

THIS IS AARON

6 Festive meals (Seudat Purim)

During the day there are lavish banquets with meat and wine, where people dance, sing, and enjoy themselves. There are also comic performances, called *Purim spiels.*

5 Masks and costumes

Purim is a great opportunity for children to dress up! Every boy wants to be the best Mordechai, every girl the most beautiful Esther. But there are all kinds of costumes in the parade.

Tanya celebrates EASTER

CHRISTOS VOSKRES! MY NAME'S **TANYA**, AND I'D LIKE TO INVITE YOU TO CELEBRATE RUSSIAN EASTER, WHICH WE CALL **PASKHA**, WITH ME. FOR US ORTHODOX BELIEVERS, THE EASTER HOLIDAYS ARE THE YEAR'S MOST IMPORTANT, AS THEY SYMBOLIZE NEW LIFE AND REBIRTH. WE CELEBRATE FOR A WHOLE WEEK, UP TO AND INCLUDING EASTER SUNDAY. EASTER COMES LATER IN RUSSIA THAN IN OTHER COUNTRIES, BECAUSE WE FOLLOW THE JULIAN CALENDAR.

1 Visits in abundance

Over the course of this week we see plenty of friends and relatives, with whom we exchange Easter gifts. Hooray!

2 Kulich (Easter bread)

I also really like *kulich*, a sweet bread made with raisins, nuts, and egg. We have it blessed in the church, along with the *paskha*, our festive dish named after the holiday.

3 Dyeing eggs

On Saturday I love to help my mom dye eggs. Not only is it fun, it's also a meaningful tradition. Different colors symbolize different things. We dye Easter eggs with onion skins.

10 Lamb

As the lamb is a traditional symbol of Easter, my mom prepares roast lamb every year for our festive meal.

a procession around the church

4 Church bell

Throughout the week anyone can go to the church and ring its bell. This symbolizes the celebration of Christ's Resurrection.

⑨ Cutting up an egg

When the whole family is gathered around the table, it is traditional to cut up an egg. It is cut into as many pieces as there are people sitting at the table, so that everyone gets a slice.

⑧ Christ is risen indeed!

Did you notice how I greeted you? *Christos voskres!* It's a traditional greeting that means "Christ is risen!" It is answered with, "He is risen indeed!"

an icon

a samovar

THIS IS
TANYA

⑦ The Orthodox church

It's important to go to church on Easter. On Saturday the priest at church blesses eggs and other food with holy water. On Sunday, we visit friends and greet each other with three kisses on the cheek.

⑥ Rolling eggs

Rolling eggs down a hill is really fun! A winning egg reaches the foot of the hill the fastest. This year my brother won—hooray!

⑤ Paskha: a festive dish

No table is complete without traditional goodies, such as paskha. Paskha is made from curd cheese in the shape of a pyramid, and it bears the letters XB (*Christos Voskrese*). The festive meal after Mass brings to an end a forty-day fast, during which time we don't eat certain foods, so we really look forward to it.

Kiyan celebrates KUMBH MELA

WELCOME TO INDIA, AND TO OUR KUMBH MELA CELEBRATIONS! MY NAME'S **KIYAN**, AND I'M GOING TO BE YOUR GUIDE. YOU COULD EASILY GET LOST HERE, AS IT'S THE BIGGEST RELIGIOUS GATHERING IN THE WORLD, ATTENDED BY MILLIONS OF PEOPLE. WE CELEBRATE THE VICTORY OF THE GODS OVER DEMONS. THE MAIN EVENT IS A PURIFYING DIP IN THE RIVER GANGES.

10 Huge numbers of people

So many people take part in the celebrations that on the main day the site can be seen from satellites in space!

1 Processions

Before we get the chance to bathe, we watch a procession of holy men enter the river in a precisely determined order. Others may go into the river only after these men have done so.

a clay pitcher

tent city

THIS IS **KIYAN**

2 Tent cities

Look how huge this tent city is! The pilgrimage takes place three times a year in four holy cities; it visits each city once every twelve years. It is attended by millions of people from all over the world.

3 Candles on the water

How lovely that looks! We put candles on the surface of the river, hoping that their journey will bring us luck.

9 Sadhu

Sadhus—ascetic pilgrims—are men dressed in orange. Some of them rub themselves with ashes. A sadhu is a spiritual teacher who leads a group of pilgrims, so he is the first to bathe in the river.

8 Sacred cow

We Hindus consider the cow to be a sacred animal—which is why we don't eat beef. This beautifully dressed-up cow is enjoying the party with us!

7 Cleansing bath

The biggest event of the whole holiday is a ritual cleansing bath. All Hindus should go to a holy river to wash away their sins, thus allowing them to live a better life. *Brr-rr!* This water's cold!

6 Hindu temple

See that temple in the distance? It's a Hindu one, and it's where we go to pray.

a cleansing bath

4 Songs

When so many people get together, there's a really happy atmosphere. Our celebrations include the singing of songs. When I sing, I dance too.

5 Pitcher

A clay pitcher called a *kumbha* symbolizes the nectar of immortality. In mythology this jar was the prize for the gods who battled with the demons. Today the festival takes place in the four places where a drop of the nectar fell.

17

Nima celebrates VESAK

WEI SAI JIE KUAILE! MY NAME'S **NIMA**, AND I'D LIKE TO WELCOME YOU TO SINGAPORE, WHERE WE'RE CELEBRATING VESAK, ONE OF THE MOST IMPORTANT BUDDHIST HOLIDAYS. WE CELEBRATE THREE EVENTS IN THE LIFE OF THE BUDDHA—HIS BIRTH, HIS ENLIGHTENMENT, AND HIS DEATH. ALL OF THESE OCCURRED IN MAY, WHEN THE MOON WAS FULL, WHICH IS WHY WE CELEBRATE THEM THEN. THE FESTIVITIES ARE CONNECTED WITH GENEROSITY, MERRYMAKING, AND LIGHTS.

1 Buddhist flags

The Buddhist flag is wonderfully colorful. But did you know that each color has a special meaning? The colors of the flag have been chosen to represent the colors of the Buddha's aura when he achieved enlightenment.

2 Buddhist monk

During the festivities we go to Buddhist temples, where we listen to monks as they recite the Buddha's words, urging us all to be peaceful and tolerant.

9 Donations for the poor

As we wish everyone happiness on this day, we give help to those who otherwise wouldn't be able to celebrate the holiday.

buddh
flag

lotus flower

3 Flowers and incense sticks

Believers place small gifts next to statues of the Buddha. These include flowers and incense sticks, which symbolize the transience of all things.

8 Candlelit procession

In the evening, after it gets dark, we join the procession with our parents. I love this part of the festivities. Everyone holds a candle, making the procession a wonderful spectacle.

7 Setting birds free

As a symbol of the liberation of the imprisoned and oppressed, we release birds, insects, and animals from captivity. I love this custom!

6 Vegetarian food

During Vesak we eat only vegetarian food. As meat is produced by killing, we do without it. The food tastes great nevertheless.

5 Buddha statue

Our parents take us to a temple where there is a statue of the Buddha in a pond. By pouring water over this statue, a believer cleanses his own karma.

4 Lotus flowers

What a lovely sight! The pond is covered with lanterns in the shape of lotus flowers. These symbolize awakening from ignorance.

THIS IS
NIMA

19

Carlos celebrates INTI RAYMI

HOLA! IT'S JUNE, AND WE'RE IN THE MIDDLE OF OUR INTI RAYMI FESTIVITIES. THE **SUN FESTIVAL** IS AN ANCIENT INCAN HOLIDAY THAT WAS BANNED IN THE 16TH CENTURY. DESCRIPTIONS OF IT SURVIVED, THOUGH, AND IT WAS BROUGHT BACK IN 1944. ALTHOUGH IT USED TO LAST TWO WEEKS, TODAY IT LASTS ONLY FOUR OR FIVE HOURS. OUR INTI RAYMI FOLKLORIC PERFORMANCES AND PROCESSIONS OF PEOPLE IN TRADITIONAL DRESS ARE SO AMAZING THAT IT'S NO WONDER TOURISTS COME FROM ALL OVER THE WORLD TO SEE THEM!

remains of Cuzco

1 Cuzco (Sacsaywaman)

The celebrations take place in Cuzco, Peru, once the center of the Incan Empire. Although nothing remains of the empire but ruins, the rituals, processions, and dances that are held in its open spaces are a great tourist attraction.

2 Winter solstice

The holiday falls on June 24th, which we in the Southern Hemisphere consider the winter solstice. Although in the past the goddess Inti was celebrated, now we celebrate St. John the Baptist Day (In the Northern Hemisphere, St. John's Day is celebrated on June 21st).

3 Sacrificing a llama

In the years of the Incan Empire the festivities included the ritual slaughter of a llama, a sacrifice that was supposed to ensure a good harvest the following year. These days—thank goodness—this is done out of sight of tourists. *Phew!*

THIS IS **CARLOS**

9 Female Incan ruler

No ruler can govern on his own, so the parade includes his wife—who is also an esteemed Incan ruler.

8 Incan ruler

A parade of actors in costume carries the Incan ruler at its head, in the place of honor. As he leads the procession, the ruler prays to the sun god.

7 Sacred coca leaves

The sacred coca leaf tells the future of the nation, so it's just as important to the celebrations as the dancing.

a llama

6 Dancers

I love to watch the dancers as they sing and move to the accompanying music. Their traditional dress brings your eyes out on stalks!

5 Masks and costumes

There are lots of different costumes. My favorite is the colorful Aya Uma mask of the leading dancer.

4 Sharing food

During the holiday we eat together and share our food. We remember our ancestors, who came to the celebrations from many places and tasted food from different regions, just as we do now.

Fatima celebrates EID AL-FITR

SELAMAT IDUL FITRI! MY NAME'S **FATIMA**, AND I'D LIKE TO WELCOME YOU TO INDONESIA. FOR US MUSLIMS, RAMADAN—THE PERIOD OF FASTING—HAS JUST ENDED. NOW THE **'SUGAR FEAST'** IS HERE, AND WE'RE ALL LOOKING FORWARD TO SEEING OUR FAMILY FOR A MAGNIFICENT MEAL AND THREE DAYS OF MERRYMAKING. EVEN DURING THIS TIME, THOUGH, WE REMEMBER OUR PRAYERS AND HELP OTHERS. ME AND MY FRIENDS ARE PARTICULARLY FOND OF THIS FESTIVAL—SO MANY SWEET TREATS AND A FIREWORKS DISPLAY IN THE EVENING!

9 Mosque

We go to the mosque to worship God, who we call Allah. At this time, we say special holiday prayers there.

1 A different route

As we go from mosque to mosque for holiday prayers, we take a different route than usual, as is recommended.

2 Fireworks

As this is an official holiday, cities often mark it with a fireworks display. We kids are particularly fond of this!

giving food to the less fortunate

3 Food as alms

Shortly before the end of Ramadan we give food (like rice, dates, grain, maize, and raisins) to charities and the poor. This allows everyone to celebrate the holidays together.

THIS IS **FATIMA**

8 Gifts

During the holidays my friends and I go from house to house in the neighborhood and sing greetings for some sweet rewards. At home we get small gifts or colored envelopes with money inside.

7 Music and dance

I really enjoy the celebrations, because there's so much merrymaking, singing, and dancing. And the food's amazing!

mosque

9

5

8

6

1

6 Sweet treats

We don't call this the sugar holiday for nothing! In the course of the day we taste many sweet things and sugary dishes.

5 Festive meals

Having fasted for a month, we really look forward to this meal. After morning prayers, we have only a light breakfast, the better to enjoy our magnificent dinner. We visit friends and relatives and wish one another good health and Allah's blessing.

4 A new dress

My mom has bought me a new dress. For the holidays we all dress up and decorate our homes.

23

Mohammed celebrates EID AL-ADHA

EID MUBARAK! WE'RE IN THE SQUARE, BY THE MOSQUE WHERE WE PRAY DURING THE EID AL-ADHA (**FESTIVAL OF THE SACRIFICE**) HOLIDAY. IN THE MUSLIM CALENDAR IT FALLS ON THE TENTH DAY OF THE LAST MONTH. ON THIS HOLIDAY—WHICH WAS DEVISED BY THE PROPHET MOHAMMED—ARABS REMEMBER THE STORY OF IBRAHIM'S DEVOTION.

9 Pilgrimage to Mecca

It is the duty of every Muslim to make a pilgrimage to Mecca once in his or her life. Millions of believers go there every year, and their pilgrimage ends with this holiday.

1 Ibrahim

I learned the story of Ibrahim from my grandfather. Although Ibrahim was prepared to sacrifice his own son for God's sake, in the end a sheep was sacrificed in the boy's place. The story reminds us, among other things, that human sacrifice is rightly forbidden.

2 One third for the poor

The meat is divided into thirds—the first for the poor and needy, the second for friends, the third for the festive meal for our family and loved ones.

THIS IS **MOHAMMED**

3 Time off

Many adults and children don't go to school or work while the holiday is in progress. So we have plenty of time to make all our preparations, and also to pray and meet with friends and family.

8 Crowded square

Prayer is an integral part of the celebrations. My father and I go to the mosque. Before we enter it, we spread a carpet under ourselves and take off our shoes. Then we pray with the others.

mosque

praying men

7 Thorough hygiene

During the holidays we must keep our bodies absolutely clean. For this reason, we wear new clothes.

6 Kissing the hand

We pay many visits at this time, to friends as well as relatives. Non-Muslim friends are welcome, too. It is traditional for us to kiss the hand of elderly people when we meet them.

5 Going to the cemetery

This is also a time for remembering our ancestors, so we visit family graves to honor their memory.

4 Truck loaded with sheep

See that truck filled with sheep? It's taking them to the butcher, as every wealthy family has a duty to buy a sacrificial animal. The meat is then shared out so that everyone can take part in the holiday.

Saanvi celebrates DIWALI

SHUBHAH DEEPAVALIHI! JOIN US AS WE CELEBRATE DIWALI, ONE OF THE MOST IMPORTANT HINDU FESTIVALS, WHICH TAKES PLACE AT THE END OF OCTOBER AND THE BEGINNING OF NOVEMBER. WE ALSO CALL IT THE **FESTIVAL OF LIGHTS**, BECAUSE WHILE IT'S GOING ON THERE ARE LIGHTS EVERYWHERE. CONNECTED WITH THE FESTIVAL ARE SEVERAL STORIES OR MYTHS IN WHICH GOOD ALWAYS TRIUMPHS OVER EVIL. DURING THE FIVE-DAY FESTIVITIES, WHICH ABOUND WITH COLOR, WE MEET UP WITH FAMILY AND FRIENDS. WE KIDS ESPECIALLY LOVE THIS HOLIDAY, AS WE RECEIVE SMALL PRESENTS.

1 Floral wreaths

During the festivities we dress in colorful, festive clothing. Children make decorative floral wreaths.

2 Mela (fair)

At this time there are *melas* (fairs) all over India. We find entertainment there, as well as things to buy. The fair is held in an open space that is decorated with lanterns, and it's really colorful.

9 Sending greetings

During this holiday, it is traditional for us to send postcards and greetings cards to our relatives and friends.

oil lamps

3 Clean homes

Before the holiday, we clean and repair our homes from top to bottom, and we put up decorations. When this is done, we open the windows and light a lamp inside, so that the goddess Lakshmi will find us.

8 Something sweet

It's polite to give friends and relatives a small gift, such as something sweet or dried fruit.

7 Rangoli

We decorate our homes by creating beautiful, colorful patterns on the floor, using dyed rice flour or sand. These patterns are greetings to divine visitors, and they bring us luck.

6 Fireworks

Today, lights are made by fireworks as well as oil lamps. Munching on something sweet while watching a firework display—I can't think of anything better!

THIS IS
SAANVI

8

2

3

rangoli

7

5 Statue of Lakshmi

Lakshmi, the goddess of wealth, fortune, and prosperity, descends to Earth only on this day. We light our homes so that she will find her way to us and we will suffer no hardship in the year to come. We honor Lakshmi by carrying a statue of her in a procession through the streets.

4 Diya

It is traditional for us to light candles in holders made of clay—small oil lamps called *diyas*. These symbolize the victory of good over evil, and also the light within us. According to our stories and myths, the light frightens away demons. We light these lamps for the goddess Lakshmi, too.

Juan celebrates DAY OF THE DEAD

HOLA! MY NAME'S **JUAN**, AND I'D LIKE YOU TO JOIN ME IN CELEBRATING **DÍA DE MUERTOS—THE DAY OF THE DEAD**. THIS IS WHEN WE MEXICANS TRADITIONALLY CELEBRATE OUR ANCESTORS. WE BELIEVE THAT ON NOVEMBER 1–2 DEPARTED SPIRITS BRIEFLY RETURN TO THE WORLD. ALTHOUGH OUR CELEBRATIONS HAVE SOMETHING IN COMMON WITH ALL SOUL'S DAY, OUR HOLIDAY IS FAR MORE COLORFUL AND CHEERFUL. IT IS BASED ON A TRADITION SO ANCIENT THAT IT IS ALMOST 3,000 YEARS OLD. ROMAN CATHOLICS ONCE TRIED TO END THESE FESTIVITIES, BUT THEY FAILED. TODAY'S FESTIVITIES HAVE AZTEC AS WELL AS CHRISTIAN ELEMENTS.

9 Papel picado

Decorations on street-side and home altars include cut-outs in fine paper. Birds, flowers, and skeletons are popular designs.

1 Body in a coffin

The parade includes someone in a coffin disguised as the deceased. This person tries to grab all the goodies and flowers that are thrown at them from the street.

2 Street-side ofrenda

An *ofrenda* is a street-side altar. We've got something like it at home, dedicated to a departed relative. We decorate it with his favorite things—photos, flowers, and candles. As we remember him, we tell amusing stories and eat his favorite food.

THIS IS
JUAN

3 Calaca

There are skeletons—called *calacas* in Spanish—and skulls everywhere! Mom and I have decorated our house with calacas, wooden skeleton figures. These are funny and very colorful, and many of them even have a musical instrument. They don't scare me at all—in fact, they make me smile.

8 Cempasúchil

Graves, altars, and masks are typically decorated with the cempasúchil flower. It's so colorful that it lights everything up!

Can you find me in the parade? There are skeletons, ghosts, and skulls everywhere. But the atmosphere is merry, and everything's so colorful! It's all part and parcel of the celebrations: we treat death as part of life.

6 Pan de muerto

A sweet roll called *pan de muerto*—'bread of the dead'—is a symbol of this holiday. Although it is sold in many stores, no one bakes it quite like my mom!

calaca

masked parade

5 Visiting the cemetery

On this day we go to the cemetery, where we tend our family's graves to the sound of church bells. In the evening, we return with our families to the now beautifully decorated graves, for a picnic—and we pray, sing, and talk.

4 Sugar skull (alfeñique)

Everywhere you turn there are lots of other goodies, too, such as decorated sugar skulls and marzipan and chocolate candy in the form of skulls, bones, and skeletons.

Kaitlyn celebrates HALLOWEEN

HAPPY HALLOWEEN! MY NAME'S **KAITLYN**. LET ME WELCOME YOU TO IRELAND, THE COUNTRY WHERE HALLOWEEN HAS ITS ROOTS. IT'S AN ANCIENT CELTIC TRADITION: IN THE PAST, PEOPLE BELIEVED THAT SPIRITS RETURNED TO EARTH ON THIS DAY (OCTOBER 31ST); SO THEY DRESSED IN VARIOUS COSTUMES AND LIT FIRES AND CANDLES IN ORDER TO DRIVE THEM AWAY. MANY OF THE OLD TRADITIONS ARE STILL OBSERVED, ALTHOUGH TODAY WE DO THIS FOR FUN!

9 Colcannon

Every year Mom prepares a traditional, simple dish called *colcannon*, which consists mainly of potatoes and cabbage. Coins are often hidden in it, to bring the finder luck. Cross your fingers that I'll find one!

1 Trick or treat

More than anything, I look forward to going around our neighbors' homes in search of sweets. At every door we ask 'Trick or treat?' in the hope that we'll be treated.

2 Ghost stories

Halloween isn't all about laughter, though. It needs to be scary, too, so it includes spooky decorations and costumes and, most important of all, the telling of ghost stories!

Jack-o-lantern

THIS IS
KAITLYN

3 Soul cakes

Sweet things are essential to the festivities. As well as the candy we get from our trick-or-treating, we bake cakes at home. These 'soul cakes' are often decorated with a cross made of raisins.

8 A cat

Pumpkins aren't the only adornments in our homes; we also have decorations in the form of skeletons, spiders, and black cats. We consider cats to be closely associated with witches.

7 Bonfires

Also seen in Ireland around Halloween are bonfires, which have long been used to ward off evil spirits and bad luck. There is also a legend connected with this: Throw a lock of your hair into the bonfire and you'll see the face of your true love in the flames. At home, we make do with a fire in the hearth.

6 Irish flag

Do you know how Halloween reached America? It came from Ireland, of course! During the 19th century, many Irish fled to America because of the potato famine, taking their customs with them.

5 Jack-o-lantern

A jack-o'-lantern is a carved pumpkin with a candle placed inside it. The name refers to Jack, a drunkard from Irish legend who managed to fool the devil and thus avoid going to Hell. A sinner, he couldn't get into Heaven—so ever since he died, his soul has wandered the world, its way lit by a cinder in a carved turnip.

4 Snap apple

Halloween is such fun! We always have a good laugh when we play the apple game. An apple is hung on a string from a line. The winner is the one who bites into it first, without using their hands.

Tony celebrates THANKSGIVING

HAPPY THANKSGIVING! MY NAME'S **TONY**, AND I'M GOING TO TAKE YOU THROUGH THANKSGIVING, WHICH FALLS ON THE FOURTH THURSDAY IN NOVEMBER. THE WHOLE FAMILY GATHERS FOR THIS HOLIDAY. WE ENJOY BEING TOGETHER, AND WE GIVE THANKS FOR ALL THE GOOD THINGS WE HAVE RECEIVED DURING THE YEAR.

9 Decorations

See how beautifully decorated our room is! I helped Mom create the new décor. We wanted to make it as pretty as possible for this festive day.

1 Pumpkin pie

Every great meal is followed by a dessert. The most popular Thanksgiving dessert in our home is pumpkin pie. Other families prefer apple pie or pecan pie.

THIS IS **TONY**

2 Football

Football is an inseparable part of Thanksgiving. We all watch important games on TV, cheering for our favorite team. Dad even wears a football jersey!

3 Whole families together

Before the holiday, the roads and airports get pretty busy—everyone wants to celebrate with their family. Before the festive meal begins we give thanks for all that is good in our lives.

8 A secular holiday

In earlier times, Thanksgiving was a religious holiday, when people gave thanks to God. Today, however, it's also celebrated by non-believers. Everyone celebrates Thanksgiving, no matter what they believe or don't believe in.

7 Food drives

On this day, too, we think of those who aren't fortunate enough to celebrate Thanksgiving as we do. Many people help out in food banks, which provide free food for all who need it. My family donates to the food bank every year.

turkey decoration

6 Parades

Every year there are Thanksgiving parades in the streets. The most famous of these is in New York. Many people come to watch and admire enormous balloons of famous storybook characters.

5 The First Thanksgiving

According to the story of the first Thanksgiving, Native Americans helped European pilgrims survive the winter by sharing their food, after which the newcomers supposedly held a dinner for the Native Americans—to thank them for their help. While the story is mostly a myth, and the reality was much harsher, especially for the Native Americans, the holiday helps us be thankful.

4 The turkey

At every Thanksgiving dinner there is a turkey with stuffing, cranberry sauce, and sweet potatoes. As such a huge quantity of turkeys is eaten at Thanksgiving, our president grants one a symbolic pardon.

Hannah celebrates HANUKKAH

HANUKKAH SAMEACH! MY NAME'S **HANNAH**, AND I'D LIKE TO WELCOME YOU TO OUR HOME. YOU'VE CAUGHT US AS WE CELEBRATE HANUKKAH, ONE OF THE MOST IMPORTANT JEWISH HOLIDAYS. WE ARE COMMEMORATING THE MACCABEAN REVOLT AGAINST ENEMIES OF THE JEWS OVER 2,000 YEARS AGO, AND THE REDEDICATION OF A DESECRATED TEMPLE THAT FOLLOWED THE VICTORY. THE FESTIVITIES LAST EIGHT DAYS, DURING WHICH WE LIGHT CANDLES ON THE MENORAH, SING SONGS, PLAY GAMES, AND ENJOY OUR TIME TOGETHER.

1 Shamash

The candles of the menorah may not be lit with matches. The shamash is an extra candle used to light all the others. Candle-lighting is a beautiful family ceremony. My dad usually lights the candle while the rest of us feast our eyes on what he is doing.

2 Gifts

During Hanukkah, people give each other presents; we children get the most. It is also traditional for us to be given a little money.

9 Women

Tradition dictates that women refrain from working during the holiday. In this way we commemorate Judith and Hannah, who inspired the Maccabean Revolt.

THIS IS

HANNA

3 Doughnuts and potato pancakes

Because we celebrate a miracle performed with oil, during Hanukkah we enjoy dishes prepared in oil. My favorites are potato pancakes and doughnuts!

8 Songs

Every night we light a candle, saying a blessing while we do so. Then we sing a song—most often *Ma'oz Tzur'* ('Mighty Rock') or *'Hanerot Halalu'* ('These Lights').

7 A dreidel

During Hanukkah we play with a four-sided dreidel (a small spinning top), betting pennies on each turn. The outcome depends on which letter is facing up after each spin. Players take turns spinning it.

candle-lighting

songbook

6 Star of David

The Star of David is a symbol of Judaism that represents balance. It also appears on the flag of Israel, our country.

5 Non-Jewish guests

During the Hanukkah festivities we invite non-Jewish guests into our homes, so that they may share in our joy and light. We want everyone to be joyous and have a good time together.

4 The Menorah

Over the eight days of the festivities we gradually light the eight candles of the menorah, which is placed by a window or the front door of our home so that the joy may spread. This is how we commemorate the miracle that followed the victory, when a single oil lamp burned for eight days rather than the usual one; this eight-day period provided for the production of new oil, allowing the Jews to rededicate the temple.

How Kids Celebrate Holidays Around the World
Authors: Helena Haraštová, Pavla Hanáčková
Illustrator: Michaela Bergmannová

© B4U Publishing for Albatros,
an imprint of Albatros Media Group, 2021.
5. května 1746/22, Prague 4, Czech Republic.
Printed in China by Leo Paper Group.
ISBN: 978-80-00-06130-6

www.albatrosbooks.com